TO:

FROM:

THE SPIRIT OF

Christmas

THE SPIRIT OF

Christmas

Contents

INTRODUCTION

The spirit of Christmas begins and ends with God and with His only begotten Son. When we make the Christmas season a time of worship and praise, we humbly acknowledge the priceless gifts that are ours through the sacrifice of our Savior, Jesus Christ. But sometimes, the hustle and bustle of the holiday season threatens to obscure the true meaning of Christ's birth. On such occasions, we must slow down, catch our breath, and consider the real reason for this glorious season. This little book is intended to help.

Are you caught up in the annual buildup that inevitably precedes December 25th? If so, please pause to consider the Bible verses and quotations that appear on the following pages. When you do, you'll be reminded that the genuine spirit of Christmas has little to do with material gifts but everything to do with spiritual ones.

May this holiday season be a time of thanksgiving and reflection for you and yours. And may the real spirit of Christmas transform your lives today and forever.

A Child is Born

For God so loved the world that He gave His only begotten Son,
that whoever believes in Him should not perish
but have everlasting life.
John 3:16 NKJV

*The story of the first Christmas
is told with breathtaking beauty
in the King James Version
of the second chapter of Luke:*

And it came to pass in those days, that there went out a decree from Caesar Augustus, that all the world should be taxed....And all went to be taxed, every one into his own city. And Joseph also went up from Galilee, out of the city of Nazareth, into Judea, unto the city of David, which is called Bethlehem, (because he was of the house and lineage of David,) to be taxed with Mary his espoused wife, being great with child.

And so it was, that, while they were there, the days were accomplished that she should be delivered. And she brought forth her firstborn son, and wrapped him in swaddling clothes, and laid him in a manger; because there was no room for them in the inn.

And there were in the same country shepherds abiding in the field, keeping watch over their flock by night. And, lo, the angel of the Lord came upon them, and the glory of the Lord shone round about them; and they were sore afraid.

And the angel said unto them, Fear not: for, behold, I bring you good tidings of great joy, which shall be to all people. For unto you is born this day in the city of David a Saviour, which is Christ the Lord. And this shall be a sign unto you; Ye shall find the babe wrapped in swaddling clothes, lying in a manger.

And suddenly . . .

. . . there was with the angel a multitude of the heavenly host praising God, and saying, Glory to God in the highest, and on earth peace, good will toward men.

Luke 2:1-14 KJV

The secret of the Christian is that he knows
the absolute deity of the Lord Jesus Christ.

Oswald Chambers

Infinite, and an infant. Eternal, and yet born of a woman.
Heir of all things, yet the carpenter's son.

C. H. Spurgeon

On Christmas Day two thousand years ago,
the birth of a tiny baby in an obscure village
in the Middle East was God's supreme
triumph of good over evil.

Charles Colson

Christmas is about a baby, born in a stable,
who changed the world forever.

John Maxwell

The Son of God does not want to be seen and found in heaven.
Therefore He descended from heaven to this earth
and came to us in our flesh.

Martin Luther

Christ is born so that, by His birth, He might restore your nature.

St. Peter Chrysologus

Jesus said . . .

If anyone thirsts, let him come to Me and drink.

John 7:37 NKJV

I am the door: by me if any man enter in, he shall be saved,
and shall go in and out, and find pasture.

John 10:9 KJV

I am the vine, you are the branches.

John 15:5 NKJV

In the world you will have tribulation;
but be of good cheer,
I have overcome the world.

John 16:33 NKJV

In every Christian, Christ lives again.
Every true believer is a return to first-century Christianity.

Vance Havner

Christ is no Moses, no exactor, no giver of laws,
but a giver of grace, a Savior; he is infinite mercy and goodness,
freely and bountifully given to us.

Martin Luther

The Son of God became man to enable men to become sons of God.

C. S. Lewis

The old message
"For unto you is born this day in
the city of David a Savior which is
Christ the Lord"
is still the heart of Christmas.

Peter Marshall

Away in a Manger

Away in a manger, no crib for a bed,
The little Lord Jesus lay down his sweet head.
The stars in the sky looked down
where He lay,
The little Lord Jesus, asleep on the hay.

The cattle are lowing, the baby awakes,
But little Lord Jesus, no crying he makes.
I love Thee, Lord Jesus!
Look down from the sky,
And stand by my cradle till morning is nigh.

Anonymous

A PRAYER

Heavenly Father, during this Christmas season, keep me mindful
of Your priceless gift: Christ Jesus. Dear Lord, You loved me before
I was ever born, and You will love me throughout eternity.
In return, let me offer my life to You so that I might live according
to Your commandments and according to Your plan. I give thanks
for Your Son Jesus and for Your everlasting love.

Amen

The Spirit
of Christmas

I will put My Spirit in you, and you shall live . . . .
Ezekiel 37:14 NKJV

The Christmas Story begins in a faraway land: a babe is born, and the world is forever changed. And, if we are to celebrate Christmas as God intends, then we, too, must be forever changed.

Christ's message is a transforming message. May we carry that message to the world, not just on Christmas day, but on every day of the year. And may the Christmas spirit, which was born with a babe in Bethlehem, dwell forever in our hearts.

The Christmas message is delivered—
the message of the light of the world
which breaks through from above,
always from above.

Karl Barth

For I am persuaded that neither death nor life,
nor angels nor principalities nor powers,
nor things present nor things to come,
nor height nor depth, nor any other created
thing, shall be able to separate us
from the love of God which is
in Christ Jesus our Lord.

Romans 8:38-39 NKJV

Christ, the Son of God, the complete embodiment of God's Word,
came among us. He looked on humanity's losing battle with sin
and pitched His divine tent in the middle of the camp
so that He could dwell among us.

Beth Moore

Christ's excellency is always fresh and new, and it delights
as much after it has been seen for ten thousand years
as when it was seen the first moment.

Jonathan Edwards

For the Son of man is come
to save that which was lost.

Matthew 18:11 KJV

Take my yoke upon you, and learn of me;
for I am meek and lowly in heart:
and ye shall find rest unto your souls.
For my yoke is easy, and my burden is light.

Matthew 11:29-30 KJV

Has he taken over your heart?
Perhaps he resides there, but does he preside there?

Vance Havner

God wants to change our lives—
and He will, as we open our hearts to Him.

Billy Graham

Christ's work of making new men is not mere improvement,
but transformation.

C. S. Lewis

If we have the true love of God in our hearts,
we will show it in our lives.
We will not have to go up
and down the earth proclaiming it.
We will show it in everything we say or do.

D. L. Moody

O little town of Bethlehem,
How still we see thee lie,
Above thy deep and dreamless sleep,
The silent stars go by;
Yet in thy dark streets shineth
The everlasting Light,
The hopes and fears of all the years
Are met in thee tonight.

O holy Child of Bethlehem!
Descend to us we pray;
Cast out our sin and enter in,
Be born in us today.
We hear the Christmas angels
The great glad tidings tell;
O come to us abide with us,
Our Lord Emmanuel!

Phillips Brooks, 1867

A PRAYER

Dear Lord, make me a joyful Christian, not just on Christmas day,
but every day of the year. Let me tell the story of Your Son,
not just at Christmastime, but in every season of the year.
Let me be Your generous, loving, faithful servant,
today, tomorrow, and forever.

Amen

A Christmas to Remember

I thank my God upon every remembrance of you.
Philippians 1:3 NKJV

Paul's letter to the Philippians was written from prison, yet the tone of the letter was joyful and triumphant. In addressing the Christians at Philippi, Paul observed that he thanked God every time he remembered his distant friends. And so it should be for us: when we think of distant friends and family members, we, too, should thank our Lord for our families, for our friends, and for our cherished memories.

We can make this Christmas a memorable one by sharing God's love and His message with all who cross our paths. When we do, we honor the Father and the One whose birth we celebrate.

Christmas, like God, is timeless and eternal.

Dale Evans

Memories of hymns and carols
keep the spirit of Christmas fresh.

Norman Vincent Peale

Happy, happy Christmas,
that can win us back to the memories
of our childhood days, recall to the old man
the pleasures of his youth, and transport
the traveler back to his own fireside
and quiet home!

Charles Dickens

Every good gift and every perfect gift is from above
and comes down from the Father of lights.

James 1:17 NKJV

The heavens declare the glory of God;
and the firmament showeth his handiwork.

Psalm 19:1 KJV

Praise the LORD, all you Gentiles!
Laud Him, all you peoples!
For His merciful kindness is great toward us,
and the truth of the LORD endures forever.
Praise the LORD!

Psalm 117 NKJV

A PRAYER

Thank you, Dear Lord, for precious memories
of Christmases past. Help me to make this Christmas
a memorable celebration of the birth of Your Son.
Amen

A Time for Family and Friends

If we love one another, God abides in us . . . .
1 John 4:12 NKJV

At Christmastime, we gather together with family and friends to celebrate the joys of the season. And, when we share our holidays with those we love, we make memories that last a lifetime.

This Christmas, too, is an opportunity to make memories for ourselves, for our families, and for our friends. May those memories be as joyful as the season we celebrate.

No other structure can replace the family. Without it,
our children have no moral foundation. Without it,
they become moral illiterates whose only law is self.

Chuck Colson

It is a reverent thing to see an ancient castle or building
not in decay, or to see a fair timber tree sound and perfect.
How much more beautiful it is to behold an ancient and noble family
that has stood against the waves and weathers of time.

Francis Bacon

A Christmas family-party!
We know of nothing in nature
more delightful!

Charles Dickens

The family circle is the supreme conductor of Christianity.

Henry Drummond

Cherish your human connections: your relationships
with friends and family.

Barbara Bush

The best times in life are made a thousand times better
when shared with a dear friend.

Luci Swindoll

In friendship, God opens your eyes to the glories of Himself.

Joni Eareckson Tada

How good and how pleasant it is
For brethren to dwell together in unity!

Psalm 133:1 NKJV

A PRAYER

Dear Lord, I am blessed to be part of the family of God
where I find love and acceptance. You have also blessed me
with my earthly family. Today, Father, I give thanks for my family
and for my friends. May the love and acceptance that I give
to them be a reflection of the love and acceptance
You have shown for me.
Amen

A Season for Thanksgiving

Rejoice evermore. Pray without ceasing. In every thing give thanks:
for this is the will of God in Christ Jesus concerning you.
1 Thessalonians 5:16-18 KJV

Sometimes, in the crush of holiday season, we simply don't stop long enough to pause and thank our Creator for the countless blessings He has bestowed upon us. But, when we neglect our God, we rob ourselves of the joy He intends for our lives.

God has blessed us beyond measure, and we owe Him everything, including our praise. Let us praise Him always, and let us thank Him for the gift of His Son.

It is only with gratitude that life becomes rich.

Dietrich Bonhoeffer

A child of God should be a visible beatitude for happiness
and a living doxology for gratitude.

C. H. Spurgeon

In everything give thanks;
for this is the will of God in Christ Jesus for you.

1 Thessalonians 5:18 NKJV

Why wait until the fourth Thursday in November?
Thanksgiving to God should be an everyday affair.
The time to be thankful is now!

Jim Gallery

Thanks be to God for His indescribable gift!

2 Corinthians 9:15 NKJV

Christmas is a good time to take stock of our blessings.

Pat Boone

The only real blind person at Christmastime
is he who has not Christmas in his heart.

Helen Keller

At Christmas, surroundings do not matter because
the spirit of Jesus is everywhere,
knocking on the doors of our hearts.

Norman Vincent Peale

Bless the LORD, O my soul,
and forget not all his benefits.

Psalm 103:2 KJV

A PRAYER

Heavenly Father, Your gifts are greater than I can imagine.
May I live each day with thanksgiving in my heart and praise
on my lips. Thank You for the gift of Your Son and for
the promise of eternal life. During this season, let me share
the joyous news of Jesus' birth, and let my life be
a testimony to His love and to His grace.

Amen

A Time for Giving

God loves a cheerful giver.
2 Corinthians 9:7 NKJV

The thread of generosity is woven—completely and inextricably—into the very fabric of Christ's teachings. If we are to be disciples of Christ, we, too, must give freely of our time, our possessions, and our love. During the Christmas season and throughout the year, we are called upon to be cheerful, generous, courageous givers. The world needs our help, but even more importantly, we need the spiritual rewards that God bestows upon us when give cheerfully and without reservation.

Christmas day is a day of joy and charity.
May God make you very rich in both.

Phillips Brooks

Let us not grow weary while doing good,
for in due season we shall reap if we do not lose heart.

Galatians 6:9 NKJV

And above all things have fervent charity among yourselves:
for charity shall cover the multitude of sins.

1 Peter 4:8 KJV

He who has two tunics, let him give to him who has none;
and he who has food, let him do likewise.

Luke 3:11 NKJV

I say to you, inasmuch as you did it to one
of the least of these My brethren,
you did it to Me.

Matthew 25:40 NKJV

Let us give according to our incomes,
lest God make our incomes match our gifts.

Peter Marshall

Since you cannot do good to all, you are to pay special regard
to those who, by the accidents of time, or place, or circumstances,
are brought into closer connection with you.

Saint Augustine

Somehow not only for Christmas
But all the long year through,
The joy that you give to others
Is the joy that comes back to you.

John Greenleaf Whittier

It is the duty of every Christian to be Christ to his neighbor.

Martin Luther

The rich man who gives to the poor does not bestow alms
but pays a debt.

St. Ambrose of Milan

Freely you have received, freely give.

Matthew 10:8 NKJV

We are never more like God
than when we give.

Chuck Swindoll

A PRAYER

Father, Your gifts are priceless. You gave Your Son Jesus to save us, and Your motivation was love. I pray that the gifts I give to others will come from an overflow of my heart, and that they will echo the great love You have for all of Your children.

Amen

A Season of Celebration

This is the day the LORD has made;
We will rejoice and be glad in it.
Psalm 118:24 NKJV

The words on the previous page, taken from Psalm 118, remind us that today, like every other day, is a cause for celebration. God gives us this day; He fills it to the brim with possibilities, and He challenges us to use it for His purposes. The day is presented to us fresh and clean at midnight, free of charge, but we must beware: Today is a non-renewable resource-once it's gone, it's gone forever. Our responsibility, of course, is to use this day in the service of God's will and according to His commandments.

On Christmas Day, we have special cause to celebrate: the birth of the Christ child. Let us praise God for His gift of His Son and the gift of this day. Both are priceless.

Merry Christmas to you!
May the glory that we celebrate
in this Christmas season fill
your life forever and ever.

Norman Vincent Peale

Have your heart right with Christ, and he will visit you often,
and so turn weekdays into Sundays, meals into sacraments,
homes into temples, and earth into heaven.

C. H. Spurgeon

To God be the glory; great things He hath done!
So loved He the world that He gave us his son.

Fanny Crosby

Jesus: the proof of God's love.

Philip Yancey

Rejoice evermore. Pray without ceasing. In every thing give thanks: for this is the will of God in Christ Jesus concerning you.

1 Thessalonians 5:16-18 KJV

Rejoice and be exceedingly glad, for great is your reward in heaven.

Matthew 5:12 NKJV

A PRAYER

Dear Lord, You have given me so many reasons to celebrate.
During the Christmas season and throughout the year,
let me choose an attitude of cheerfulness. Let me be
a joyful Christian, Lord, quick to laugh and slow to anger.
And, let me share Your goodness with my family, my friends,
and my neighbors, this day and every day.

Amen

Through the Eyes
of a Child

Suffer the little children to come unto me, and forbid them not;
for of such is the kingdom of God.
Mark 10:14 KJV

Christmas is a special time for children. As the big day nears, youngsters become more and more excited about the prospects of the big day. And as adults, we can learn from their excitement.

Materialism, of course, is a sign of spiritual immaturity, but joy is not. And while our children may look longingly at brightly wrapped gifts under the tree, we adults should fix our collective gaze much higher up, at the star that symbolizes that night in Bethlehem when our Savior was born. Then, with childlike exuberance, we should encourage our children to enjoy the Christmas season while keeping them ever mindful that Christ is, and always will be, the greatest Christmas gift of all.

It is good to be children sometimes,
and never better than at Christmas,
when its mighty Founder was
a child himself.

Charles Dickens

When Jesus put the little child in the midst
of His disciples, He did not tell the little
child to become like His disciples;
He told the disciples to become
like the little child.

Ruth Bell Graham

Children are the hands by which
we take hold of heaven.

Henry Ward Beecher

Let us look upon our children; let us love them and train them as children of the covenant and children of the promise. These are the children of God.

Andrew Murray

To love children is to love God.

Roy Rogers

A child is a beam of sunlight from the Infinite and Eternal.

Lyman Abbott

Every child born into the world
is a new thought of God,
an ever-fresh and radiant possibility.

Kate Douglas Wiggin

A PRAYER

Lord, the children of this world are Your children.
Let us love them, care for them, nurture them, teach them,
and lead them to You. And during this Christmas season,
as I serve as an example to the children under my care,
let my words and deeds demonstrate the love
that I feel for them . . . and for You.

Amen

God's Grace

For by grace you have been saved through faith,
and that not of yourselves; it is the gift of God, not of works,
lest anyone should boast.
Ephesians 2:8-9 NKJV

On the very first Christmas day, when God sent His Son to become the salvation of the world, He bestowed a gift that is beyond price and beyond human comprehension. We have not earned our salvation; even the best among us fall far short of God's commandments. But, when we accept Christ as our savior, we are saved by God's grace. Let us praise God for His gift, and let us share His Good News with the world.

Costly grace is the treasure hidden in
the field; for the sake of it, a man will gladly
go and sell all that he has. It is costly because
it costs a man his life, and it is grace
because it gives a man the only true life.

Dietrich Bonhoeffer

The life of faith is a daily exploration of the constant
and countless ways in which God's grace and love are experienced.

Eugene Peterson

The grace of God is infinite and eternal. As it had no beginning,
so it can have no end, and being an attribute of God,
it is as boundless as infinitude.

A. W. Tozer

Grace is not about finishing last or first; it is about not counting.
We receive grace as a gift from God,
not as something we toil to earn.

Philip Yancey

To be in a state of true grace is to be
miserable no more; it is to be happy forever.
A soul in this state is a soul near
and dear to God. It is a soul housed in God.

Thomas Brooks

But immediately Jesus spoke to them, saying,
"Be of good cheer!
It is I; do not be afraid."

Matthew 14:27 NKJV

The Christmas story gives
its triumphant answer:
"Be not afraid."

Karl Barth

A PRAYER

Dear Lord, during the Christmas season and throughout the year,
I praise You for Your priceless gifts. You have saved me by Your grace.
Keep me mindful that Your grace is a gift that I can accept
but cannot earn. Let me share the good news of Your grace
with a world that desperately needs Your healing touch.
Amen

A Time for Prayer

Watch ye therefore, and pray always....
Luke 21:36 KJV

The Christmas season is a time when we offer thanks to Jesus and to the One who sent Him. We express thanksgiving through our words, through our deeds, and through our prayers.

Jesus instructed His followers to pray always, and His advice applies to Christians of every generation. When we weave the habit of prayer into the very fabric of our days, we invite God to become a partner in every aspect of our lives. And, when we make the Christmas season a time of thanksgiving and prayer, we welcome the Christ child into our hearts, which, of course, is exactly where He belongs.

Whether we think of, or speak to, God,
whether we act or suffer for him,
all is prayer when we have no other object
than his love and the desire of pleasing him.

John Wesley

If I should neglect prayer but a single day,
I should lose a great deal of the fire of faith.

Martin Luther

Don't pray when you feel like it;
make an appointment with the King and keep it.

Corrie ten Boom

Get into the habit of dealing
with God about everything.

Oswald Chambers

If the spiritual life is to be healthy
and under the full power of the Holy Spirit,
praying without ceasing will be natural.

Andrew Murray

Wasted time of which we are later ashamed, temptations we yield to,
weaknesses, lethargy in our work, disorder and lack of discipline in
our thoughts and in our interaction with others—
all these frequently have their root in
neglecting prayer in the morning.

Dietrich Bonhoeffer

He who kneels most stands best.

D. L. Moody

The effective, fervent prayer
of a righteous man avails much.

James 5:16 NKJV

Ask, and it will be given to you;
seek, and you will find;
knock, and it will be opened to you.
For everyone who asks receives,
and he who seeks finds,
and to him who knocks it will be opened.

Matthew 7:7-8 NKJV

A PRAYER

Lord, as I we celebrate the birth of Jesus, keep me mindful that Christmas is a time for thanksgiving and prayer. I pray to You, Father, because You desire it and because I need it. Prayer not only changes things; it also changes me. Make me a prayerful Christian, Lord, and let me turn every aspect of my life over to You, today and forever.

Amen

And the Greatest of These . . .

And now abide faith, hope, love, these three;
but the greatest of these is love.
1 Corinthians 13:13 NKJV

Christmas should be a time to celebrate, a time to contemplate, and a time to share feelings of warmth and appreciation with those we love. Let's make this holiday season a Christmas to remember by expressing our love and affection for family members and friends. When we do, we make ourselves dutiful servants of the One whose birth is the reason for this glorious season.

The greatest Christmas gift
is wrapped inside the human heart;
it is the gift of love.

Marie T. Freeman

If we love one another, God abides in us, and His love has been perfected in us.

1 John 4:12 NKJV

A friend loves at all times.

Proverbs 17:17 NKJV

Since love grows within you, so beauty grows.
For love is the beauty of the soul.

Saint Augustine

Love one another fervently with a pure heart.

1 Peter 1:22 NKJV

The whole being of any Christian
is Faith and Love.
Faith brings the man to God;
love brings Him to men.

Martin Luther

Give me such love for God and men as will blot out
all hatred and bitterness.

Dietrich Bonhoeffer

Only joyous love redeems.

Catherine Marshall

Carve your name on hearts, not on marble.

C. H. Spurgeon

A PRAYER

Lord, during this season when we celebrate the birth of Your Son,
help me to show kindness to all those who cross my path,
and let me show tenderness and unfailing love to my family
and friends. Make me generous with words of encouragement
and praise. And, help me always to reflect the love
that Christ Jesus gave me so that through me,
others might find Him.

Amen

Peace on Earth

These things I have spoken to you, that in Me you may have peace.
In the world you will have tribulation; but be of good cheer,
I have overcome the world.
John 16:33 NKJV

During the holiday season, we pray for peace in our own lives and for peace throughout the world. Jesus offers us peace, not as the world gives, but as He alone gives. We, as believers, can accept His peace or ignore it. When we accept the peace of Jesus Christ into our hearts, our lives are transformed and the promise of the Christmas season is fulfilled.

Peace with God is where all peace begins.

Jim Gallery

And suddenly
there was with the angel
a multitude of the heavenly host
praising God, and saying . . .

"Glory to God in the highest,
And on earth peace,
goodwill toward men!"

Luke 2: 13-14 NKJV

He brought peace on earth and wants to bring it also into your soul,
that peace which the world cannot give.

Corrie ten Boom

The Christmas message is that there is hope for humanity,
hope of pardon, hope of peace with God, hope of glory.

J. I. Packer

Look around you and you'll be distressed; look within yourself
and you'll be depressed; look at Jesus, and you'll be at rest!

Corrie ten Boom

Silent Night! Holy Night!
All is calm, all is bright.
Round yon virgin mother and child!
Holy infant so tender and mild,
Sleep in heavenly peace,
sleep in heavenly peace.

Father Joseph Mohr, 1818

I heard the bells on Christmas Day,
Their old familiar carols play,
And wild and sweet Their words repeat
Of peace on earth, good will to men!

Henry Wadsworth Longfellow

As fits the holy Christmas birth,
Be this, good friends, our carol still—
Be peace on earth, be peace on earth,
To men of gentle will.

William Makepeace Thackery

It Came Upon a Midnight Clear

It came upon the midnight clear,
that glorious song of old,
From angels bending near the earth,
to touch their harps of gold.

Peace on the earth, goodwill to men,
from heav'n's all gracious king,
The world in solemn stillness lay
to hear the angels sing.

Edmund Sears, 1850

A PRAYER

Lord, when I turn my thoughts and my prayers to Jesus,
I am blessed. On these days when I celebrate Christ's birth,
let me welcome Him into my heart, and let me accept His peace,
not just for today, but for all eternity.

Amen

A Time for Worship and Praise

Is anyone cheerful? Let him sing psalms.
James 5:13 NKJV

Nothing should obscure the fact that Christmastime is the annual birthday celebration of the Christian faith. Christmas day is, first and forever, a religious holiday-a time for Christians everywhere to rejoice, to pray, and to worship God. During this holiday season, it is proper that we keep our eyes, our voices, and our hearts lifted upward as we offer profound thanksgiving to God through our worship and through our praise.

Praise Him! Praise Him!
Tell of His excellent greatness;
Praise Him! Praise Him!
Ever in joyful song.

Fanny Crosby

O Come All Ye Faithful

O come all ye faithful, joyful and triumphant,
O come ye, O come ye to Bethlehem
Come and behold him,
born the King of angels
O come let us adore him,
O come let us adore him,
O come let us adore him,
Christ the Lord.

Sing, choirs of angels, sing in exultation,
Sing all ye citizens of heaven above,
Glory to God, all glory in the highest,
O come let us adore him,
O come let us adore him,
O come let us adore him,
Christ the Lord.

Latin Carol, 18th Century

Make a joyful noise unto the LORD
all ye lands. Serve the LORD with gladness:
come before his presence with singing.
Know ye that the LORD he is God: it is he
that hath made us, and not we ourselves;
we are his people and the sheep
of his pasture.

Enter into his gates with thanksgiving,
and into his courts with praise;
be thankful unto him and bless his name.
For the LORD is good;
his mercy is everlasting; and his truth
endureth to all generations.

Psalm 100 KJV

Our God is the sovereign Creator of the universe!
He loves us as His own children and has provided every
good thing we have; He is worthy of our praise every moment.

Shirley Dobson

Praise-lifting up our heart and hands, exulting with our voices,
singing his praises-is the occupation of those
who dwell in the kingdom.

Max Lucado

I will praise the name of God with a song,
and will magnify him with thanksgiving.

Psalm 69:30 KJV

I was glad when they said unto me,
Let us go into the house of the LORD.

Psalm 122:1 KJV

Worship is not taught from the pulpit.
It must be learned in the heart.

Jim Elliot

Each time, before you intercede, be quiet first and worship God
in His glory. Think of what He can do and how He delights to hear
the prayers of His redeemed people. Think of your place
and privilege in Christ, and expect great things!

Andrew Murray

A PRAYER

Lord, let Christmas day and every day be a time of worship.
Whether I am in Your house or simply going about my daily
activities, let me worship You, not only with words and deeds,
but also with my heart. In my quiet moments, let me praise You
and thank You for creating me, for loving me,
for guiding me, and for saving me.

Amen

Joy to the World

These things have I spoken unto you, that my joy might remain in you,
and that your joy might be full.
John 15:11 KJV

Christ made it clear to His followers: He intended that His joy would become their joy. And it still holds true today: Christ intends that His believers share His love with His joy in their hearts.

This Christmas season let us accept the joy that is ours through the One who gave His life so that we might have life abundant and eternal.

If you who have a troubled heart,
listen to the angel's song:
"I bring you tiding of great joy!"
Jesus did not come to condemn you.
If you want to define Christ rightly,
then pay heed to how the angel defines Him:
"A great joy!"

Martin Luther

Joy is the serious business of heaven.

C. S. Lewis

When God blesses us, He expects us to use those blessings
to bless the lives of others.

Jim Gallery

The manger is a symbol of what can happen
when Jesus Christ resides in us.

Bill Hybels

Now may the God of hope fill you
with all joy and peace in believing,
that you may abound in hope
by the power of the Holy Spirit.

Romans 15:13 NKJV

The LORD reigns;
Let the earth rejoice.

Psalm 97:1 NKJV

What is your focus today?
Joy comes when it is Jesus first, others second…then you.
Kay Arthur

Gratitude changes the pangs of memory into a tranquil joy.
Dietrich Bonhoeffer

If you're a thinking Christian, you will be a joyful Christian.
Marie T. Freeman

Joy to the World

Joy to the world!
The Lord is come!
Let earth receive her king.

Let every heart prepare Him room,
and heaven and nature sing,
and heaven and nature sing,
and heaven, and heaven,
and nature sing.

Isaac Watts, 1719

Let the hearts of those rejoice
who seek the LORD!
Seek the LORD and His strength;
Seek His face evermore!

1 Chronicles 16:10-11 NKJV

When Jesus Christ is the source of our joy,
no words can describe it.

Billy Graham

God rest you merry, gentlemen,
Let nothing you dismay,
Remember Christ our Savior
Was born on Christmas day,

To save us all from Satan's pow'r
When we were gone astray;
O tidings of comfort and joy, comfort and joy,
O tidings of comfort and joy.

18th Century English Carol

Rejoicing is clearly a spiritual command.
To ignore it, I need to remind you, is disobedience.

C. H. Spurgeon

Rejoice, the Lord is King; Your Lord and King adore!
Rejoice, give thanks and sing and triumph evermore.

Charles Wesley

There is not one blade of grass, there is no color in this world
that is not intended to make us rejoice.

John Calvin

Christmas means the beginning
of Christianity—and a second chance
for the world.

Peter Marshall

A PRAYER

Lord, make me a joyous Christian. Because of my salvation
through Your Son, I have every reason to celebrate life.
During this Christmas season, let me share the joyful news
of Jesus Christ, and let my life be a testimony
to His love and to His grace.
Amen